Original title:
Branches of Banter

Copyright © 2025 Creative Arts Management OÜ
All rights reserved.

Author: Victor Mercer
ISBN HARDBACK: 978-1-80567-450-4
ISBN PAPERBACK: 978-1-80567-749-9

The Frolic of Floating Fronds

In the sun, the leaves take flight,
Tickling each other, a silly sight.
Dancing in the warm, sweet air,
Laughter bursts out everywhere.

Swaying and twisting, they play their game,
Each one teasing, yet none feel shame.
Whispers of jokes float on the breeze,
Nature's jesters, aiming to please.

Woven Words in the Breeze

Under the shade, a secret we weave,
Giggling softly, wanting to believe.
Words like butterflies, darting and play,
Tickling the moments of this sunny day.

Laughter rings out from a nearby tree,
As two squirrels bicker so comically.
Their chatter a tapestry, bright and bold,
Stories of silliness, joyously told.

Echoes of Quips and Quarrels

In the leafy boughs, a frolicsome fight,
Critters exchange their clever insight.
"Your acorn is tiny!" one tiny voice teases,
While the other retorts, "Mine's full of cheeses!"

Echoes of laughter bounce off the ground,
In this quirky kingdom, joy can be found.
With every quip, their spirits arise,
Painting the woods with their witty surprise.

Humor in the Shade of Laughing Boughs

Beneath the shade where the branches meet,
Lies a gathering place that's quirky and sweet.
A chorus of chuckles, a blend of delight,
A banquet of banter from morning to night.

Here, owls may wisecrack, and crows crack a joke,
While chipmunks brighten the air with their yoke.
In this woodland theater, the laughter won't fade,
For humor and silliness bask in the shade.

The Art of Lighthearted Spar

In the garden of giggles, we play,
With words that twist and dance like ballet.
Each quip a petal that floats in the air,
Tickling the funny bone, stripping despair.

Like playful kittens chasing a thread,
We leap into laughter, enough said.
A jab here, a jest there, all in good fun,
Our duel of wits shines bright like the sun.

With puns like blossoms, they bloom with glee,
In this cheerful clash, we're wild and free.
Each chuckle a victory, no need to spar,
In the art of lightness, we're all a star.

Conversations Under the Sky

Under the sky so wide and blue,
We toss out jokes like seeds anew.
With laughter as our celestial guide,
We sway to the rhythm, side by side.

Like clouds that drift without a care,
Our banter floats on warm summer air.
A tickle of humor, a wink and a nod,
In the sunlight's glow, we feel like gods.

Through chatter, we weave a splendid thread,
With whimsy and joy, the heart is fed.
A tapestry of giggles, bold and spry,
Crafted sweetly in moments that fly.

Jests that Swing and Sway

From a swing set high, our laughter unfolds,
With jests that shimmer like bright, shiny gold.
We spin tales spun from whimsical dreams,
Joy bouncing around like shimmering beams.

A playful nudge, a sarcastic spin,
With humor, we settle, let the fun begin.
Each punchline delivered with a playful grace,
Laughter echoing in this charming place.

Under a sun where the giggles replay,
We leap and we twirl, in an endless ballet.
When playful jests sway in rhythmic delight,
We dance through the day, hearts ever so light.

Tangles of Humor and Heart

In the knots of laughter, we find our peace,
With humor our language, our worries cease.
A twist here, a turn there, our spirits soar,
In the game of jesting, we're always wanting more.

Like vines that twirl and wrap around tight,
Our funny little tales bring all pure delight.
With each hearty chuckle, we uncover the art,
In the tangle of smiles, we mend every heart.

Through the labyrinth of jokes, we wander so free,
Finding joy hand in hand, just you and me.
Together we travel down this winding path,
With humor entwined, we escape the wrath.

Whispers of Witty Leaves

In a garden where the giggles grow,
Leaves play peek-a-boo with the sun's glow.
A raccoon in a hat, sipping sweet tea,
Says, "Who's the funniest? Come laugh with me!"

Squirrels argue about the best acorn prize,
While frogs croak jokes from clever disguise.
The breeze joins in with a cheeky hum,
As chatter and laughter begin to come.

Laughter in the Canopy

Above the world, where the silly birds sing,
A parrot cracks jokes on a shiny spring thing.
With feathers of bright, and wit on full charge,
Each quip brings smiles; it's laughter at large!

High up in the air, where secrets convene,
The owls strike poses, posing as keen.
Their wise old eyes twinkle with glee,
As they share snickers from high on the tree.

Chatter Among the Twigs

Twigs gossip softly, like whispers at night,
As robins retell their comedic flight.
They tease the young sprouts with tales of the past,
Saying their giggles must surely outlast!

A chipmunk pipes up, with mischief in mind,
Creating wild riddles, they're quite one of a kind.
The laughter erupts, a delightful ruse,
In this high-up world, with no hint of blues.

Dance of the Playful Vines

Vines twist and twirl with a joyful spin,
As laughter abounds, rat-a-tat-tat, let's begin!
They tickle the trunks with a playful embrace,
Each giggle a spark in this leafy place.

With every sway and every playful knot,
The sun joins the frolic, cheering a lot.
Dancing together, they banter and prance,
In a swirling delight, they all take a chance.

The Witty Wilderness Walk

With squirrels that chatter and chatter with glee,
They plot out their schemes, as clever as can be.
A rabbit hops by, wearing a bow tie,
Declaring a race, oh me, oh my!

The trees are all giggling, leaves rustling loud,
The mushrooms are dancing, they've formed quite a crowd.
A fox in a sweater winks at the crew,
And mimes all the jokes that he thinks will ensue.

The brook starts to babble, with tales of a fish,
Who dreamt he could fly and make a grand swish.
The crickets all laugh, they can't catch their breath,
As they tell him to stick to his water-bound depth!

Upon a high branch, a parrot takes flight,
Telling tall tales that stretch through the night.
The whole forest listens, wrapped up in his fun,
With punchlines that sparkle like rays from the sun!

So come take a stroll where the wild things all play,
In a world full of laughter, it's here to stay.
For nature's a jester, it dances and sings,
On this witty wild walk, where joy always springs!

Humor's Haphazard Harvest

In a garden of giggles we tread,
Where each chuckle fills a pot with spread.
Laughter spills from the fruits of jest,
With each silly line, we are truly blessed.

Jokes grow wild like weeds in the sun,
Tickling our ribs, oh what fun!
The more we pick, the more we find,
A harvest of humor, joyfully entwined.

We plant seeds of puns in the ground,
Watch them sprout, oh, what joy abounds!
Every grin a testament to cheer,
In this happy patch, smiles appear.

So let's gather the nuggets of cheer,
In our playful plot, we hold dear.
With jokes as sweet as ripe summer's fruit,
In this zany garden, life is astute.

The Radiant Ribbon of Riddles

Tied in knots, our thoughts collide,
A colorful thread, where laughs abide.
Questions weave through the fabric bright,
A tapestry of jest, pure delight.

Each twist and turn, a surprise unfolds,
Stories told in riddles bold.
The more we unravel, the wittier we get,
In the ribbons of laughter, we never fret.

So come, my friend, let's solve this lore,
Riddles that dance and tease to the core.
With every answer, our joy will bloom,
Wrap ourselves in humor, dispelling gloom.

With smiles stitched tight, our crew's a delight,
In this playful riddle, we take flight.
Life's a puzzle, each laugh a key,
Unlocking joy for all to see.

Silhouettes of Smiles

In shadows cast by the setting sun,
Our laughter echoes, a race to run.
Smiles take shape, a playful jest,
In the silhouettes, we find our rest.

Glimmers of joy in every face,
Creating a chorus, a silly embrace.
From frowns to grins, watch the dance,
As light and shade engage in chance.

With every giggle, the night grows bright,
Mischief dances in the moonlight.
In laughter's glow, new forms we see,
Silhouettes of joy, wild and free.

So let's shape our smiles in the dark,
Crafting memories, igniting the spark.
In this playful theatre, we act our part,
With laughter's language, we fill our hearts.

Ramblings of the Radiant

Wandering thoughts, a festive spree,
In the land of giggles, so wild and free.
Each word a sparkle, a wink, a tease,
Our ramblings dance like a gentle breeze.

Chasing after tales that twist and spin,
Where wit and whimsy together begin.
Lively chatter fills the air we share,
In this joyful chaos, love's everywhere.

We'll paint our stories with colors bright,
Scribbles of laughter, pure delight.
Puns and riddles, a playful match,
In this radiant ramble, no need to hatch.

So let us wander with smiles so wide,
In this journey, we take in stride.
With every step, we'll spin a rhyme,
In the land of laughter, we're timeless, sublime.

The Jesting Jam

In a quirky cafe, where the coffee flows,
The barista twirls, putting on a show.
With whipped cream mustaches and cups full of cheer,
Each sip comes with laughter, the best brew here.

The muffins debate, who's the fluffiest treat,
While scones roll their eyes, feeling beat.
A croissant chimes in, with a buttery grin,
In this playful jam, let the fun begin!

Riffs from the Roots

From the soil they sprout, with a giggly glee,
A pun-loving plant, oh, how funny they be!
Jokes hanging like fruit, ripe for the taking,
With chuckles as branches, there's no mistaking.

The carrots crack wise, in a playful duet,
While radishes tease, never one to forget.
In the garden of gags, sowing laughter anew,
The roots share their tales, all funny, it's true!

The Foliage of Fun

Beneath leafy canopies, the whispers delight,
As vines twist in laughter, what a marvelous sight.
The trees tell tall tales, with a rustle and sway,
Giggling in sunlight, they brighten the day.

The flowers join in, with petals aflutter,
Each bloom adds a pun, like a sweet little utter.
In this garden of glee, joy sprouts all around,
With humor as seasoning, happiness found!

Laughs in the Lattice

In a maze of woodwork, the jokes intertwine,
Frames full of quips, both quirky and fine.
The trellis leans in, with a smirk on its face,
As vines tell their stories, leaving nary a trace.

The gates creak with mirth, joining in the fun,
As shadows play tricks, in the setting sun.
Every twist and turn hides a giggle so bold,
In the lattice of laughter, pure joy to behold!

The Leafy Canvas of Camaraderie

In the park where giggles play,
Leaves rustle with what they say.
Friends toss jokes like frisbees bright,
Laughter dances until the night.

On swings, we soar with funny tales,
Navigating life like fish in gales.
Every quip a vibrant hue,
Painting skies in shades of blue.

Beneath the tree's wise, smiling bark,
We plot our pranks 'til well past dark.
With whispering winds as our cue,
We cling to laughter like morning dew.

So grab a seat upon this ground,
Where every laugh is joy unbound.
In this leafy realm, we renew,
Our bonds of jest, forever true.

Merriment Among the Mistletoe

Underneath the green and gold,
Kisses mixed with laughter bold.
Every wink, a spark of fun,
Mistletoe jokes for everyone.

With each step, a chuckle sounds,
Love and laughter swirl around.
We share our tales with merry cheer,
Holding memories we hold dear.

Every branch, a secret shared,
Surrounded by friends who truly cared.
In playful jests, we find our way,
Through tangled vines, both night and day.

So let's gather 'neath this leafy dome,
Where laughter feels so much like home.
Here we weave our joyful rhyme,
In the spirit of festive time.

The Harmony of Humorous Hues

In fields of colors bright and bold,
We paint the day with jokes retold.
With brush in hand, we splash away,
Creating laughter day by day.

Each shade a story, rich and grand,
Together, we walk hand in hand.
From silly slips to playful jests,
In this gallery, we are the guests.

The sun smiles down, a golden hue,
While clouds giggle, a fluffy crew.
In every stroke, a memory gleams,
We laugh together, chasing dreams.

So join this dance of playful grace,
In a world where joy finds its place.
With each hue, our spirits sing,
In this harmony, let laughter ring.

Swaying Sentences in the Summer Air

As breezes swirl, our words take flight,
Chasing squirrels in pure delight.
With every twist, a punchline flies,
Like kites that dance in sunny skies.

In this warm and wiggly breeze,
We share our tales with perfect ease.
Side-splitting tales that brightly bloom,
Filling the air like sweet perfume.

With every chuckle, hearts expand,
In this summer, jesting hand in hand.
The trees nod gently to our sound,
While laughter echoes all around.

So let the wind carry our mirth,
In this season, we find rebirth.
Together we sway, our joy laid bare,
Dancing on words in the summer air.

The Teasing Trellis

In the garden, vines entwine,
Whispers giggle, hearts align.
Flowers chuckle with a twist,
A potion brewed, we can't resist.

Petals toss their heads in glee,
Winking at the bumblebee.
Sunshine drips with humor bright,
Nature's jest in pure delight.

Laughter drifts on breeze so light,
As frogs croak jokes beneath the night.
Swaying branches in a dance,
Invite us all to join the prance.

So come and pluck this joy anew,
Among the leaves, a merry view.
In the garden, come and play,
Where laughter sprinkles every day.

The Amusing Assemblage

Gather round, the crew is here,
With playful banter, spread the cheer.
Mice are telling tales of cheese,
While cats chuckle, if you please.

Squirrels scamper, hide and seek,
With acorn hats, they're far from meek.
Rabbits hop with jokes in tow,
Spreading giggles, stealing show.

In this clique, each pun's a gem,
Who knew a tree could have such whim?
Laughter bubbles over like a brook,
Join the fun, take a look!

Round the trunk, with giddy glee,
A merry jaunt, just you and me.
In this haven where jesters root,
A patch of gags that never hoot.

Chortles in the Orchard

Under the trees, whispers play,
Apples chuckle in the fray.
Branches swaying, tales unfold,
As oranges grin, the stories told.

A crow cracks jokes on the fence,
While rabbits roll, their laughter dense.
The breeze carries giggles, oh so sweet,
As flowers wiggle to the beat.

The grass is green, the sun's a clown,
Tickling toes as we gather 'round.
In this orchard, hilarity bounces,
Where nature's humor truly pounces.

Grab a seat beneath the vines,
Listen close, as joy aligns.
With every chuckle, bloom a rose,
In this garden where laughter grows.

Boughs of Banter's Bouquet

In a field where laughter sways,
And every bloom has quirky ways.
Petals flutter, jokes take flight,
Beneath the stars, so warm, so bright.

The daisies peek with cheeky grins,
While sunflowers sway like they're in spins.
Around the blooms, the mischief thrives,
As butterflies share their witty jives.

A breeze delivers quips a-plenty,
With lilacs laughing, oh so gently.
In every corner, joy runs wild,
Every giggle, like a child.

So come, rejoice, bring a cheer,
In this bouquet, hold humor dear.
Nature's jest, a vibrant show,
In this realm, let laughter flow.

The Subtle Spark of Humor

In a coffee shop, a sip so sly,
A brew that tickles, oh my!
With laughter bubbling like a frothy cream,
Two pals exchange a giggling dream.

Witty jests dart, a playful throw,
As puns flit by like a card trick show.
A wink, a grin, the air is light,
Their chuckles dance into the night.

Stories tumble with a clumsy grace,
Each punchline drops, they quicken the pace.
With every chuckle, their spirits soar,
As humor opens wide the door.

So let the laughter echo, loud and clear,
For in this moment, joy is near.
A spark ignites with every quip and tease,
In the serendipity of silly memories.

Laugh Lines and Leaf Edges

Underneath the leafy spread,
Lies a story of laughter said.
Each rustle whispers a fresh delight,
A leaf falls laughing in the twilight.

With every chuckle, the sun shines bright,
Casting shadows that dance in the light.
Giggles weave through the branches high,
Tickling the clouds that float on by.

Animated tales they weave in jest,
Like squirrels, they leap at their playful quest.
With mischief sprouting from root to tip,
Jokes unfurl as the branches flip.

So gather round, let spirits rise,
Embrace the giggles, no room for sighs.
In this garden where laughter spreads,
The joy of play keeps worry at bay.

The Jocular Grove

In the jovial grove where humor stands,
Every trunk has a tale, and every branch expands.
Squirrels debate 'who eats more nuts?',
While birds chirp laughs, all in short cuts.

Beneath the old oak's gossiping shade,
Whispers of tomfoolery serenade.
A merry band, in colorful dress,
Dancing around, sharing their jest.

The ground sparkles with mischief's glow,
As creatures gather, it starts to flow.
Wit and whimsy, they intertwine,
Each line a riddle, each laugh divine.

So let's raise a cheer for the days so fine,
Where silliness rules, and jokes combine.
In this haven of humor, darkness can't stay,
For joy is robust in the light of play.

Breezes of Banter

A gentle breeze weaves through the trees,
Carrying chuckles that float with ease.
Fluffy clouds giggle up in the sky,
While shadows leap, as they too comply.

Whispers of wit twist through the air,
A jolly parade of jests everywhere.
As daisies chuckle, and daisies sway,
They bloom in laughter, leading the way.

Echoes of jesting weave bright and bold,
Spun on the spindle of stories retold.
With every tickle of the sun's warm rays,
Joyful banter ignites the days.

So slip into this carefree tide,
Where humor's the compass and giggles preside.
Let every moment be spun with glee,
In breezy jests, forever be free.

Echoes of Amusement

Laughter bounces in the air,
Jokes that twirl like wind-blown hair.
A wink, a nudge, a playful tease,
With every chuckle, the heart warms with ease.

Whispers of glee through the trees pass,
Stories shared that tickle like grass.
A waddle, a jig, the dance of delight,
In the garden of humor, all is bright.

With every twist of the tale we spin,
Each punchline lands, we cannot help but grin.
We gather round, a quirky brigade,
Where silliness thrives, and worries fade.

Laughter rings true, like bells in the night,
In this lovely chaos, everything feels right.
Conflict dissolved in animated chatter,
As joy intertwined makes the world feel flatter.

Conversation's Hidden Roots

Underneath layers of playful exchanges,
Lies a wealth of smiles, in quirky ranges.
Each banter a fruit, ripe for the pick,
In the orchard of wit, every quirk does stick.

Grins so contagious, they lighten the mood,
Like sunshine breaking through a grumpy feud.
Each comment a seed, sown with delight,
Blossoming laughter, sparkling and bright.

From puns that sprout in the spring of our chat,
To tales of mishaps, woven in spat.
We climb through the thicket, goofing around,
In this realm of mirth, true joy is found.

So let's gather 'round, where comedy flows,
With roots so deep, and humor that grows.
In this garden of jests, we'll forever thrive,
Sharing laughter, keeping the spirit alive.

The Humorous Undergrowth

Here in the thicket where laughter blooms,
We venture through giggles, with whimsical tunes.
Every rustle, a jest; every branch, a laugh,
The path of the silly is our rightful staff.

Ticklish fables weave through thick vines,
As absurdities waltz in playful designs.
With every stumble, a grin must arise,
In this forest of folly, joy never lies.

Amidst the chaos, we find our best pals,
In this undergrowth where humor enthralls.
A tumble, a jest, oh how we do thrive,
In a world of giggles, we feel so alive.

So gather your friends, let's bask in the fun,
In this whimsical patch, we all can run.
With laughter as fuel, we'll dance through the night,
In the jungle of joy, everything feels right.

Words Woven in Laughter

Threads of humor weave through our chat,
Like a cozy old sweater, imagine that!
Every pun we spin, every joke we share,
Knits us together, beyond compare.

We stitch our own tales, each loop a delight,
With threads of giggles that shine oh-so-bright.
A patchwork of quirks in a brilliant array,
Each chuckle a fabric that colors our day.

So let's spin our yarns, the zany and bold,
In this tapestry of laughter, warmth never grows old.
For every stitch tells a story anew,
In this world of jest, it's me and you.

From whispers of mirth to loud roars of cheer,
Our woven creation brings everyone near.
In this fabric of friendship, with whimsy entwined,
We celebrate life with laughter, unconfined.

Serenade of Silly Sparring

In the garden of jest, we play,
Tickling the air with every word,
Puns bounce around like a ballet,
Every chuckle a joyful bird.

With quips like butterflies in flight,
We dance through the leaves, mischief in tow,
Every glance fuels the playful fight,
In this comedy, we steal the show.

Laughter sprinkles like morning dew,
As jokes spring forth from the tree's embrace,
Crafting a world that's merry and new,
In this light-hearted, charming space.

So come join the laughter parade,
In the shade where humor will unfurl,
Together, in jest we wade,
Spinning joy in a playful whirl.

Tongue-in-Cheek Treetops

Up in the treetops, our banter flies,
Twisting and turning like playful vines,
Jests hum along with the breeze's sighs,
In this canopy, where humor shines.

A squirrel chuckles, it joins the fun,
As acorns drop like punchlines surprise,
In a world where laughter has just begun,
And each grin is a prize in disguise.

With stickers and winks, we sway and swing,
Crafting tales that bubble like gum,
Each giggle a note, a song to sing,
In our treetop stage, we come undone.

So come take a leap from branch to branch,
Where whimsy blossoms and spirits soar,
In this cheeky venue, we take our chance,
To spin stories and laughter galore.

Frivolous Flowering Talk

Amidst petals bright with playful cheer,
We chat like bees buzzing through the blooms,
Sparking laughter and giggles sincere,
In this garden where joy brightly looms.

With daisies nodding to every pun,
And roses blushing at tales we weave,
The sunflowers laugh, they've joined the fun,
In this tapestry, we gladly believe.

Tickling stems and leaves, oh what a sight,
Where humor grows taller than any vine,
Every word fluttering, light as a kite,
In this realm where we joyfully dine.

So come let's frolic in this embrace,
Where jokes sprout like petals in spring,
In the fragrance of mirth, find your place,
As we dance and laugh, let joy take wing.

The Bantering Breeze

A breeze whispers jokes through the trees,
With laughter trailing like ribbons of air,
Every gust teases, plays with such ease,
In this merry ballet, there's magic to share.

The sun plays hide-and-seek with the clouds,
As waves of chuckles ripple the field,
In the wind's warm arms, joyfully loud,
It spins tales with laughter gently revealed.

With every shift, new quips take their flight,
Like silly birds darting from branch to branch,
We dance to the rhythm, joyous and bright,
In this whimsical gale, spirits enhance.

So let's sail on this breeze of delight,
Where mirth is as carefree as the wind,
In this world of fun, pure and light,
We'll banter and laugh, till the day's end.

The Smiling Sap

In the grove where laughter grows,
Saplings chuckle, a stand-up show.
Leaves whisper jokes, the sun approves,
Nature's jesters, where humor moves.

Squirrels prank with acorn tricks,
Frogs croak punchlines, quick and slick.
Wind joins in with a gentle hum,
A symphony of smiles, oh what fun!

The babbling brook spills words that shine,
Every ripple carries a funny line.
Among the blooms, a giggle troupe,
Nature's comedy, a vibrant loop.

Even the sunlight starts to dance,
A cheeky game, a playful chance.
In this forest, joy takes flight,
A tapestry of laughter, pure delight.

Riddles in the Roots

Beneath the ground where shadows peep,
Worms tell secrets that make you leap.
Tangled tales from the dirt so deep,
Riddles tickle, laughter to keep.

Mice invent their clever schemes,
Underground parties burst at the seams.
With every burrow, a jest runs wild,
Nature's children, both funny and wild.

The stones are wise, they'll crack a grin,
Charting stories of where they've been.
Each root a punchline, winding tight,
In the soil, humor takes flight.

Giggles resonate from the earthy bed,
Where every creature's a pun-filled thread.
In riddles whispered by roots that sway,
The heart of the forest laughs all day.

Mirthful Meadow Musings

In the field where daisies dance,
Bumblebees buzz and take a chance.
They spin around with joyous glee,
A merry ballet, wild and free.

Butterflies tickle the laughing grass,
With vibrant colors, they flit and pass.
They share tales from flower to flower,
Each petal chuckles, a whimsical power.

Clouds overhead wear goofy grins,
Casting shadows where humor spins.
The sun winks bright, a cheeky light,
Chasing worries away, what a sight!

In this meadow, where silliness reigns,
Every breeze carries playful gains.
Let joy be the laughter that comes our way,
In nature's embrace, we dance and play.

The Quirky Canopy

High above in the leafy maze,
Birds tell jokes in amusing ways.
With chirps and tweets, they weave a tale,
Of silly antics that never fail.

Branches sway with an elegant flair,
Rustling whispers fill the air.
Each gust of wind brings a jest anew,
Tickling the leaves that dance and strew.

Monkeys swing with comedic grace,
Playing pranks, a wild race.
Squirrels sit upon their throne,
In the canopy, they laugh and groan.

As sunlight dapples the floor below,
Nature's laughter begins to flow.
In this quirky space where spirits gleam,
The forest giggles, a shared dream.

The Amusing Aisle

In the supermarket, a cart rolls by,
Chasing a lost balloon in the sky.
A pickle jar laughs, 'Oh, what a sight!'
As fruits start dancing, what sheer delight!

Down the cereal lane, the spoons take a bow,
While the cookies engage in a back-and-forth vow.
'I'll crumble for you!' the biscuit did say,
And the milk giggled, splashing away.

Checkout lines buzzing with joyful chatter,
As shoppers debate what's on the platter.
Some cartwheel through aisles, seeking a thrill,
While the chips chuckle, 'Now that's quite a skill!'

Laughter erupted in every aisle's nook,
As the chocolate bars plotted to cook.
They whispered sweet nothings, a mischievous game,
In this lively lane, we're never the same!

Whims of the Willows

Beneath the willows where laughter does loom,
Squirrels play pranks, causing quite the flume.
One drops an acorn, causing a cheer,
The birds mimic giggles, oh what a year!

A rabbit in glasses reads tales with glee,
While the frogs on the bank croak in spree.
'What's in a name?' a wise turtle asked,
As the hedgehogs spun tales, humor unmasked.

Leaves whisper jokes in the warm summer breeze,
A chorus of chuckles among the trees.
'Why did the berry bring a shoe?'
'To stomp all the grumbles, just like we do!'

Even the sun grinned, its rays divided,
Tickling the grass where laughter resided.
In this merry spot, where smiles abound,
The whims of the willows keep joy all around.

Joyful Juxtapositions

A cat kissed a dog, what a quirky pair,
With paws overlapping in laughter's fresh air.
In the park they pranced, tails in a twist,
Creating a scene that could not be missed.

A clown on a tricycle zoomed past with flair,
Chasing a kite caught up in the air.
The children all giggled, 'What's going on?'
As the giggling gusts of wind danced along.

Sidewalk painters splashed colors with zest,
While pigeons performed, an unplanned fest.
'Hey, where's our food?' a duck quacked in haste,
As they gathered for crumbs no longer laid waste.

In this wild world where contrasts do greet,
Rabbits to turtles—an unusual feat.
Joyful juxtapositions, a laugh and a grin,
In nature's great folly, we all can join in!

Witty Wilderness Wanders

In the woods where the laughter runs free,
A fox cracked a joke about bees in a tree.
The bear, with a cackle, rolled down a hill,
While the owls stifled hoots, soaked in the thrill.

A chipmunk juggled acorns with glee,
While raccoons played cards, sipping fresh tea.
'This hand's a winner!' one shouted with pride,
As the trees shook their leaves, the laughter supplied.

Even the brook joined in the fun,
With splashes and tickles under the sun.
'Why cross the road?' asked a goose in a row,
'To get to the laughter; now that's how we flow!'

Witty wilderness, a comedy show,
Where creatures collide with a friendly hello.
With each step we take, unexpected delight,
The forest is buzzing in pure day and night!

The Art of Playful Parley

In the garden where laughter sprouts,
Two friends share giggles, no doubts.
With every word, the sunshine glows,
Tickling thoughts where humor flows.

A jest about a stubborn shoe,
That couldn't keep up, oh who knew?
They laugh until their sides are sore,
With every quip, they crave for more.

Witty repartees take their flight,
Underneath the stars so bright.
Each punchline dodges and weaves,
In this world of joyful leaves.

In the artful spacing of their glee,
Every chuckle, wild and free.
For in the game of playful chat,
They're the jokers, imagine that!

Jests in the Shade

Beneath the tree, a raucous crowd,
With quips that ring so very loud.
One jokes about a fluffy cat,
Who thinks it's cool to wear a hat.

They trade the tales of daily fights,
With laundry visiting on bright nights.
Each pun a leaf that rustles clear,
Filling the air with shouts of cheer.

A silly dance breaks out, oh dear,
As branches sway, their hearts sincere.
The shade a canvas, bright and bold,
Where laughter's woven, stories told.

In every chuckle, they unite,
With misshaped rhymes that don't feel right.
Yet in this light, they find their aim,
To turn the mundane into a game.

Dialogue's Dancing Leaves

Where leaves twist to a merry tune,
Conversations drift like a balloon.
Each word a flutter, bright and free,
As laughter dances in the greenery.

One quips of toast that won't stay put,
Another brags of their best foot.
With every line, they twist and twirl,
In this leafy laugh-out-loud whirl.

Jokes scatter like confetti warm,
With butterfly wit, they form a storm.
As each pun lands, the echoes swell,
In stories woven, all is well.

Between the boughs, the mirth takes flight,
In bursts of joy that feel so right.
For within this dialogue's embrace,
They find delight, their happy place.

Chatter in the Canopy

Up high, where whispers bubble light,
The chatter spins in pure delight.
With jests that coil like vines around,
The humor grows, all around.

A tale of socks that lost their mate,
And cooking fails that turned out great.
Laughter floats like petals tossed,
In this canopy, they're never lost.

Their words a tapestry so grand,
Each punchline sown by cheerful hand.
As giggles drift on breezy trails,
In the rhythm of their playful scales.

Together weaving, thick as thieves,
Tales that dance on playful leaves.
In this leafy stage, they play their part,
With every joke, they share their heart.

Parodies in Poles

A squirrel tried to make a call,
But ended up stuck in a mall.
With acorns here and nuts all there,
He danced around without a care.

The pigeons plotted on a plan,
To steal a french fry from a man.
They feigned a war, a feathered fight,
Then flew away, what a delight!

The ducks quacked tunes, a soggy choir,
In hopes to catch a laughing sire.
While frogs croaked beats from lily pads,
They beamed with joy, it wasn't bad!

A walrus wobbled with a laugh,
Deciding on the perfect half.
He slipped and slid, what a big fuss,
But in the end, he rode the bus!

The Rooted Revelry

Beneath the leaves, a raccoon played,
In search of snacks, he wasn't swayed.
He wore a hat, quite bold and loud,
Declared himself the chef for this crowd.

The rabbits clapped with joyful cheer,
As he whisked up more snacks, oh dear!
A pie made of dandelion greens,
Made everyone laugh, what silly scenes!

A turtle slow with jokes to tell,
Kept cracking puns, oh how they fell!
The trees giggled with leaves that swayed,
While critters gathered, unafraid.

At dusk, they danced in the cool night air,
Creating shadows without a care.
In their own world, they enjoyed the fun,
Underneath the big old sun!

Upbeat Understory

In the underbrush, so wild and free,
Frogs and crickets planned a spree.
They donned bright hats, with stripes galore,
And boogied down near the old oak door.

A beaver brought his favorite drum,
As beetles marched, oh what a hum!
With twirling leaves and flickered lights,
They laughed and danced through summer nights.

A ladybug won the hula game,
Spinning round, she earned her fame.
While fireflies twinkled in delight,
Joining the fun, lighting up the night!

The party raged till morning sun,
A burst of joy, oh what a run!
In cozy nooks, they'd rest and dream,
Of next year's laughter, oh what a theme!

Cheery Chatter

Atop the hill, a pair sat down,
Two squirrels plotting, both wore a frown.
They schemed for laughs, a nutty prank,
In search of jokes like a treasure bank.

A fox walked by, with ears quite perked,
He heard the giggles, and then he smirked.
With a flip of his tail, he joined the fun,
Jokes were shared till the day was done.

The chattering birds chirped in too,
With silly quips and a comedic view.
Their banter bounced from branch to branch,
As hedgehogs rolled in, lost in a trance.

When twilight came, they spread the cheer,
Sipping dew drops, toasting their year.
With friends gathered all around the glen,
They'd share these giggles again and again!

Laughing Leaflets

In the garden, whispers fly,
A ladybug with a curious eye.
Tickled by the breeze, they dance,
Nature's jesters in a merry trance.

Squirrels swap tales of acorn theft,
While blossoms nod, feeling quite deft.
Petals blush at a butterfly's flit,
Life's a joke, and they're loving it!

Giggles rise from daisies bright,
As bees buzz around in pure delight.
Winking at clouds that drift and sway,
Funny moments in the light of day.

Leaves chuckle softly, a rustling sound,
In this lively patch, joy is found.
With every rustle and every cheer,
Nature's laughter brings us near.

Parables among Petals

Tulips tell tales of a rainy night,
While roses giggle at a butterfly's flight.
"Did you see that clumsy bee?" they chime,
Buzzing around like it's playtime!

Daffodils rustle, sharing their dreams,
Winning at life, or so it seems.
The world's a stage where blooms perform,
In the sunniest of times, it's the norm.

Breeze carries secrets from one to another,
"You won't believe what happened, my brother!"
Flirting flutters, petals in a whirl,
A humor-filled dance in this floral swirl.

Sunflowers grin at the passing parade,
While daisies plot a playful charade.
Nature's laughter, a beautiful sound,
In this garden, joy knows no bound.

Riffs among the Reeds

Whistling winds through the grassy blades,
A symphony of jokes the river wades.
"Did you hear what the catfish said?"
Laughter echoes where the reeds are spread.

Frogs croak puns from their lily pad throne,
Each joke delivered with a hilarious tone.
The dragonflies giggle, darting with flair,
Creating a ruckus in the warm night air.

Crickets chirp riffs, a song in the dark,
Witty retorts from the feisty lark.
With every splash, there's a chuckle, a cheer,
Life by the water, so wonderfully clear.

The reeds sway softly, as if in a jest,
Nature's orchestra, we're all feeling blessed.
In this vibrant patch where laughter thrives,
The sound of joy, truly comes alive.

Mirthful Murmurs

In city parks where the grass grows thick,
Pigeons gossip with a comical kick.
"Did you see her strut?" one bird quips,
As they ruffle their feathers, sharing their trips.

Children laugh, chasing after the breeze,
While dandelions spread with the greatest of ease.
"Make a wish!" they chant, oh so loud,
In this whimsical scene where joy is unbowed.

Trees shake their leaves, gossiping away,
"Can you believe what the wind did today?"
Laughter rings through branches and cores,
As nature chuckles, and the fun restores.

With every rustle, a tale unfolds,
Of giggles and grins as the day beholds.
In this merry world of playful cheer,
The spirit of joy is forever near.

Jive among the Limbs

In the trees where squirrels play,
They dance and tease all day,
A nutty tale is spun,
While branches sway, having fun.

The owls hoot with a wink,
As acorns roll, they think,
The leaves laugh, a rustling song,
Echoes here where jokes belong.

A woodpecker taps a beat,
While critters gather, oh so sweet,
The sun peeks through, a playful glow,
As laughter rises, soft and low.

In this forest, where joy's a friend,
Each whispering leaf, a giggling trend,
Nature's jesters, bold and bright,
Share their jive from morn till night.

Musing in the Meadow

In a field where daisies sway,
Bees buzz jokes, all in play,
Butterflies join the fun parade,
As sunlight dances, unafraid.

Frogs croak puns with glee,
While ants tell tales, one, two, three,
A breeze carries giggles high,
As clouds float by and wink an eye.

Each flower bends to hear the jest,
Nature's humor, simply the best,
With petals fluttering in delight,
A meadow of smiles, pure and bright.

The bugs join in with a chirpy cheer,
With every laugh, they draw us near,
In this lush haven, laughter seeds,
Sprout joyfully from all our needs.

Puns in the Petals

Roses whisper, 'Look at me!'
Tulips tease with glee, oh, see!
Petals flutter, laughter rains,
As colors burst, delight no chains.

Daffodils tell a joke or two,
'What's yellow and shines? It's you!'
Sunflowers nod with giddy grins,
As blossoms laugh, the fun begins.

Pollinators buzz, a jolly crew,
With tongue-in-cheek, they join the view,
In this garden of clever rhymes,
Nature's humor defies the times.

With fragrant pranks, they intertwine,
Each bloom a pun, a clever line,
In petals bright, the laughter blooms,
Sprinkling joy like sweet perfumes.

Giggles on Grapevines

In vineyards lush, the grapes all smile,
Together giggling, all the while,
Vines entwined in a joyful dance,
A party of fruit, given the chance.

The tendrils tease and play a game,
As sunlight bathes them without shame,
A squirrel dances on a vine,
While crickets chirp, their jokes align.

Each cluster laughs, a sight to see,
As shadows stretch in jubilee,
With every sip from nature's cup,
The world joins in, lifting us up.

In this vineyard, joy fills the air,
A grapevine's jest, beyond compare,
With every burst, a laugh divine,
Become a toast, as we entwine.

The Witty Wilderness

In the forest where chuckles grow,
Trees whisper secrets, stealing the show.
Squirrels debate, with acorns in tow,
While laughter sparkles, a vibrant glow.

The owls roll their eyes, wise and discreet,
As raccoons craft jokes that can't be beat.
Branches sway gently, to a rhythm so sweet,
In this merry land, all mischief's a treat.

Nature's a jester, a playful old chap,
With vines that tangle like a funny mishap.
Every rustle and giggle wraps us in a wrap,
While shadows dance lightly, a whimsical map.

Golden rays filter through leaves of bright green,
Casting funny shapes in the spaces between.
In this world of glee, it's the laughter we've seen,
That's sprouted like flowers, so silly and keen.

Saplings of Sarcasm

Little sprouts laugh at the taller trees,
With pokes and jibes carried on the breeze.
'Look at the trunks!' they tease with such ease,
As the giants just sigh, their patience a squeeze.

In the garden, where giggles abound,
One tiny bloom claims to know all the sound.
'I'm the queen of humor, I wear the crown!'
While daisies and daisies roll on the ground.

The sun beams down, with a wink and a smile,
As butterflies flutter, to stay for a while.
Mirth bubbles up, it's a jovial style,
Filling hearts with joy, running life's hectic mile.

Roots intertwine, forming laughter's embrace,
In this playful patch, no frowns find their place.
Nature's sarcasm sets an endless pace,
Where every odd line paints a brightened space.

The Enchanted Exchange

In a clearing where giggles flit,
Creatures convene—oh, what a wit!
A rabbit tells tales, with a wise old split,
While the fox rolls his eyes, 'Heavens, not this skit!'

The mushrooms applaud, all in a fuss,
As the parrot swings by, making a fuss.
'Keep it classy, fellas, without all the muss!'
Creating a ruckus, a laugh-inducing thrust.

Even the brook joins, with a bubbly cheer,
Waves of water giggle, so crystal-clear.
It whispers to stones, "What a charming frontier!"
In this festival of laughter, joy draws near.

Twilight approaches, with jokes in the air,
Nature's comedians, everywhere fair.
In laughter's embrace, we lose all our care,
In this enchanted exchange, we're light as a hare.

Frolics in Foliage

Winds nudge the leaves, sending tickles of cheer,
As branches gossip, their tales we revere.
Flowers burst forth, a colorful sphere,
Painting the laughter that floats through the clear.

A deer tries to dance, in a jovial spin,
With missteps aplenty, but joy's what they win.
Under the bright sun, where troubles grow thin,
Every leaf echoes, let the fun begin!

The clouds play hide and seek, in a playful guise,
While bunnies trade quips, that leave us in sighs.
In this merry meadow, where whimsy complies,
The forest throws parties that never say goodbyes.

Laughter rings high, from the roots to the sky,
In frolics of foliage, oh my, oh my!
Where every green corner seems ready to try,
To sprinkle a giggle, as time flutters by.

The Breezy Exchange of Friendly Quips

In a park where the laughter flies,
Jokes hang like fruit in the sky.
Friends trading barbs, a playful race,
Each smile a prize, each grin a place.

A wink shared here and a nudge there,
Silly stories dance in the air.
Under the sun, they let words flow,
Tickles and giggles, a vibrant show.

A pun leaps forth like a frog on a quest,
With each clever jab, they're truly blessed.
Rolling in gales of pure delight,
Their jests a melody, taking flight.

Through laughter's echoes, they weave and spin,
A tapestry of joy, where all can win.
At dusk, the quips gently fade away,
But friendships bloom in the fading day.

Clouded Conversations in a Sunlit Grove.

Beneath the leaves where the shadows play,
Chatter bubbles bright, come what may.
An umbrella of smiles in the shade,
As sunny remarks gleefully cascade.

With every jest, the world feels light,
A symphony of laughter, pure delight.
They trade their tales like summer fruit,
Beneath the branches, they share the loot.

One slips on words, another chimes in,
Like dancing leaves in the breeze, a twin.
With playful nudges, the moments they seize,
Each witty line is a gentle tease.

In this sunny grove where shadows roam,
The heart finds a rhythm, a perfect home.
As giggles twirl in the golden hue,
They craft their tales, both old and new.

Whispers of Witty Exchange

In the quiet nook where secrets thrive,
Humorous whispers come alive.
Each jest a pebble tossed with glee,
Creating ripples, wild and free.

A sly wink signals a clever quip,
As laughter sails on a friendship's ship.
With every pun, the night ignites,
Stars above join in, giggling delights.

Their words dance lightly like fireflies,
Lighting up the night with playful ties.
Every chuckle a thread clearly sewn,
In this tapestry, they've brightly grown.

Soft echoes of fun fill the air,
No room for seriousness, only flair.
Bound together through jovial sound,
In the grove of laughter, joy is found.

Laughter's Twisted Vines

In the garden where quirks entwine,
Laughter blooms on each vine.
With tangled thorns, they play their part,
Every joke a tickle to the heart.

Through pointed leaves and jests so sly,
They find the punchline to defy.
With playful banter wrapped so tight,
A riot of humor in the fading light.

Giggling fruits hang just so low,
While witty words together grow.
A playful breeze flutters all around,
In a maze of laughter, joy is found.

At day's end, as the sun retreats,
Their fun remains in rhythmic beats.
With memories climbing like twisted vines,
Their laughter echoes, love aligns.

Folly in Full Bloom

In a garden where laughter spills,
The daisies dance, ignoring thrills.
A squirrel prances with a nutty grin,
While bees hum tunes that make us spin.

Frogs croak symphonies of delight,
As butterflies flutter, oh what a sight!
The sun winks down with a playful glare,
In this vibrant realm, there's fun in the air.

Each petal's joke is a jest so sweet,
Even the weeds can't handle the heat.
With giggles echoing, joy is a bloom,
In the folly of flowers, there's always room.

So come join this fest, leave troubles behind,
In this charming spot, pure laughter you'll find.
As nature's jesters all take a bow,
In folly's embrace, let's revel, and how!

The Waggish Woods

In woods where shadows come to play,
The trees whisper secrets throughout the day.
A fox tells tales of mischievous nights,
While owls hoot softly, sharing delights.

Beneath a canopy of quirky cheer,
The squirrels plot, holding their beer.
Beneath the boughs, laughter ignites,
As acorns fall, like playful bites.

Rabbits hop in the merry parade,
While raccoons wear masks, a comical charade.
With every rustle, a joke takes flight,
In waggish woods, hearts feel so light.

So let's dance with shadows, twirl with the leaves,
In this woodland gala, where laughter believes.
The waggish woods invite us to roam,
With chuckles and fun, it's our nature home!

Threads of Lightheartedness

In the loom of life, we weave our thread,
With colors of laughter, joy widespread.
Each stitch a giggle, each knot a cheer,
In the tapestry of fun, we have no fear.

With every twist, a story unfolds,
Of clumsy moments and antics bold.
The fabric of friendship, so warm and bright,
Threaded with chuckles, a pure delight.

Through the patterns of jest, we find our way,
In this lighthearted quilt where we play.
A patchwork of smiles, stitched with cheer,
Wrapped in the warmth of those we hold dear.

So raise a toast to this wacky design,
With threads of joy that forever align.
In the art of laughter, we find our place,
In the weave of lightheartedness, embrace!

Jesting in June

In the sunny month where mischief grows,
We gather for laughter, as everyone knows.
Picnics and pranks fill the warm air,
With lighthearted jesters, there's fun everywhere.

Children's giggles echo with glee,
As ice cream melts, sticky as can be.
A puppy in shades struts down the lane,
Causing the passersby to chuckle and strain.

Under bright umbrellas, jokes take flight,
As fireflies come out to dance in the night.
Frolicking friends chase the setting sun,
In jesting June, we're all on the run.

So let's celebrate this month of delight,
With laughter and fun, we'll dance through the night.
As stars twinkle softly, our spirits will soar,
In jesting June, we're always wanting more!

Quirks Among the Foliage

In the garden of giggles, they dance with cheer,
Where leaves trade jests, and no one's austere.
A sunflower winks, a bemused rose sighs,
While daisies tell jokes that make bumblebees cry.

Petunias play pranks with a fluttering tone,
While the ivy entwines, feeling funny, alone.
The oak throws his voice, deep and profound,
As the lily pads whisper, 'Oh, look who's around!'

Squirrels in laughs, with a nutty delight,
While the wind carries chuckles, pure joy in the light.
Even the snails, dressed in their shells,
Chime in the humor, with their slippery spells.

No serious thoughts, just a bright, merry show,
Where laughter's the rain, and the smiles grow.
Each petal and leaf, in this playful display,
Breathe out the joy, chasing shadows away.

Unruly Sprigs of Sarcasm

The willow's too dramatic, with a sighing refrain,
While the cactus just laughs, oh what a pain!
'Can you believe it?' shouts the feisty hedge,
As roses declare, 'We'll lead, don't you edge.'

A dandelion grins, with a mischievous dare,
'I'm fluffier than clouds, and I don't need a care!'
The thyme rolls its eyes, in a herbal retort,
As the lilacs debate, while the daisies cavort.

Beneath the broad oak, the swiper bug shouts,
'Not that leaf again! I'm tired of your bouts!'
The fun never fades in this leafy parade,
Where each little sprig has its own masquerade.

Quick wit intertwines through this green tapestry,
From the smallest of petals to the grandest of tree.
Their laughter resonates, a chaotic delight,
As the sun sets on stories shared in the light.

A Symphony of Silly Sprouts

Down in the garden, we all find our place,
With giggles galore and the silliest face.
The carrots wear hats, the cucumbers dance,
While the broccoli jokes if they stand a chance.

In rows, they all mingle, in soil they confide,
Each sprout with a quirk, bursting with pride.
The pumpkins tell tales, quite large and round,
As the herby chorus sings soft, with no sound.

The cabbage declares, 'I'm the best of the bunch!'
And peas scatter laughter, a colorful punch.
The sunflowers roll over, with petals in glee,
Inviting the clouds for a wild jamboree.

So wander through gardens, where joy's in the air,
With sprouts full of antics, there's light everywhere.
In a symphony crafted by nature's own hand,
Each plant joins the laughter, in bright, silly band.

Folly in the Ferns

Among the soft ferns, where shadows play tricks,
A party of laughter, with sly little flicks.
Each frond has a story, a jest up its sleeve,
In this secretive grove, where all can believe.

The mushrooms are nodding, in caps they collide,
While the bluebells assert, 'We won't let it slide!'
A critique from the moss, with a grin on its face,
Says, 'Oh, but dear ferns, you're a tangled disgrace!'

Laughter spills freely on this leafy retreat,
With gossiping petals, the fun's bittersweet.
'Who wore it best?' asks a gnarled, wise vine,
As the daisies all giggle, perfectly fine.

With folly in the ferns, the laughter won't quit,
In this green little realm where every joke's lit.
Take heed, take a chance, join the rustic display,
For in the garden's mischief, we chase blues away.

The Whimsy of Weaving Words

In the garden of chatter, we sprout,
Words do a jig, with laughter about.
Puns bloom like flowers, bright and bold,
Tickles our toes, a sight to behold.

Jokes dance on branches, swaying in glee,
Twisting like vines, so wild and free.
Each giggle a petal, a burst of delight,
We weave our tales deep into the night.

Lively exchanges, they flutter and play,
Every wisecrack brightens the day.
From silly to clever, a playful caress,
Our garden of gags, a comedy mess.

With every quip, a giggle grows near,
Nestled in laughter, we shed all our fear.
So come join the fun, let your worries unwind,
In this joyful forest, free and unconfined.

Giggling Leaves of Laughter

Whispers of humor rustle the trees,
Tickling the branches, with playful ease.
Laughter erupts, like rain on the ground,
Giggling leaves dance, twirling around.

Each chuckle's a breeze, sweeping through skies,
A jolly parade, where nonsense flies.
In the shade, we share tales that twist,
With every punchline, none can resist.

Silly anecdotes flutter like kites,
Soaring high, bringing pure delights.
From witty comebacks to jabs so sly,
Echoing joy, let our spirits fly.

In this rustling stage, all hearts align,
In whimsical woods, where humor's divine.
So gather your buddies and let laughter bloom,
In the giggling grove, we'll banish the gloom.

Sunshine of Snarky Sentiments

Sassy remarks like rays in the morn,
Shining a light, on humor reborn.
With wit as our guide, we venture ahead,
In the garden of jests, no tears will be shed.

Jabs wrapped in smiles, oh what a treat,
Burning with sass, never knowing defeat.
We blossom like daisies, bright and absurd,
Words weave a melody, sweetly unheard.

In a sunbeam of banter, we find our groove,
Snappy replies make us bust a move.
Every eye-roll a petal, soft and spry,
In this floral arena, we'll reach for the sky.

So bask in the warmth of our playful exchange,
With sunshine and giggles, nothing feels strange.
Together we flourish, like vines intertwined,
In the glow of snark, true joy we will find.

Lighthearted Growth in Gloom

When shadows loom, we wear silly grins,
Making the best of where laughter begins.
Witty repartees sprout from the dark,
Lighting our paths, igniting a spark.

Underneath clouds, our spirits still thrive,
With cheeky remarks, we feel so alive.
Sprinkled with humor, the rain turns to cheer,
Chasing the moody clouds far from here.

In a garden of giggles, we dive and we sway,
Dancing through puddles in a joyful ballet.
With friends by our side, we weather the storm,
Creating our sunshine, a brand new norm.

So while the world frowns and the skies seem gray,
We'll build our own laughter, come what may.
In lighthearted growth, we'll always find bloom,
Turning melancholy into a room full of zoom.

Lively Lingering Laughter

Under the sun, we giggle and play,
Witty remarks light up the day.
With poking jests, we tease and cheer,
Laughter echoes, bringing good cheer.

Tales so tall, they twist and turn,
In every jest, there's much to learn.
Funny faces and silly grins,
In the dance of humor, everyone wins.

From whispers soft to roaring shouts,
Each quip pulls more into the bout.
Beneath the shade, we share our glee,
Creating memories, wild and free.

So raise a glass to the joy we share,
In this whirlwind of laughs, we lay bare.
With every chuckle, our spirits soar,
In this merry world, who could ask for more?

Dialogue's Leafy Layers

Beneath the boughs where chatter thrives,
Words tumble out and laughter dives.
In the branches of tales grown tall,
We pluck the best, we heed the call.

Each playful poke, a joyous spark,
In the heart of talk, we leave our mark.
A swirl of giggles, connections bloom,
In this wacky world, there's always room.

Chasing thoughts from tree to tree,
Every twist of phrase entertains the spree.
With quips like leaves that dance in the breeze,
Together we wander, our hearts feel at ease.

So gather round for more delight,
With every chuckle, the mood ignites.
These fragrant exchanges, forever to savor,
In the garden of friendship, we find our flavor.

The Joyful Network

In the net of jokes, we're all entwined,
With each punchline, new humor we find.
Witty webs that twist and weave,
In every word, there's love to believe.

Signals flying through the air,
Bouncing off with laughter to share.
Each light-hearted jest, a link in time,
Creating memories, sublime and prime.

With smiles as bright as the morning sun,
In this network of joy, we frolic and run.
Catch the giggles, throw them wide,
Here, in this web, all troubles slide.

So let the laughter roll like waves,
In this joyful current, we are brave.
Connected by humor, hand in hand,
Crafting a symphony, oh so grand!

Jocular Journeys

Pack your bags, it's time to roam,
With silly stories, we make it home.
Each step we take, a chuckle, a cheer,
On this journey, there's nothing to fear.

Lost in laughter, under the sky,
With whimsical tales that float on high.
We ride the waves of glee and fun,
In the jesting sun, our smiles outrun.

From quaint coffee shops to quirky fairs,
Every corner turned, laughter declares.
With comic tales that bend, not break,
In the happiest moments, memories awake.

So let's travel far on this comedic quest,
In the garden of giggles, we find our rest.
For every good joke is a treasure, it seems,
As we spin around in our laughter-filled dreams!

The Lighthearted Arbor

Under the tree, laughter takes flight,
Squirrels join in, what a silly sight.
Leaves whisper secrets, giggles galore,
Nature's own stage for jokes to explore.

A crow tells a tale, it's quite absurd,
A frog leaps in, and it's all a blur.
The sun beams down, casting shadows wide,
Every little chuckle, a joy to abide.

Frolicsome breezes tickling our toes,
While ants hold a meeting, who really knows?
Lively banter among the lush green,
This merry place feels like a dream.

As dusk drapes softly on this playful scene,
We gather round, hearts light and keen.
The stars peek down, joining our cheer,
In this joyous arboreal sphere.

Quips upon Twigs

On a twig, a bird cracks a silly pun,
His feathered friends chuckle, oh what fun!
A squirrel rolls by, nuts in a stash,
He joins the jest, it's quite a splash!

Beneath the leaves, a game starts to brew,
A rabbit hops in with humor anew.
The wind carries laughter, sweet and bright,
Under this bough, everything feels right.

A deer walks past, quite unsure what's said,
Yet still he joins in, tilting his head.
With every flicker, the giggles grow loud,
The trees sway gently, a laughter crowd.

Twigs drip with joy, and the world seems light,
As shadows grow longer, we banter in flight.
Nature's own theater, with mirthful delight,
Each quip a reminder of purest delight.

Banter Beneath the Boughs

In the shade, where jokes take root,
A chipmunk jives, in a tiny suit.
With every nut tossed, laughter flies high,
Beneath the boughs, spirits swim in the sky.

Old owls hoot with wit most grand,
Sharing tales of their adventures, so unplanned.
A butterfly flutters, joins in the fun,
Adding her sparkle, like beams from the sun.

The blossoms are bright, swaying to the beat,
While bumblebees dance, oh what a treat!
In this cheerful grove, none wear a frown,
We trade our quips, wearing laughter's crown.

As twilight approaches, our laughter won't end,
For in every leaf, there's a new friend.
Under the vastness, in joy we remain,
Bantering softly, till it starts to rain.

The Playful Pathways

Along the pathway, where giggles abound,
We stroll side by side, humor unbound.
A path lined with pokes, good-natured jest,
In this jubilant walk, we find our best.

The rustle of branches sings loud and clear,
As critters conspire, delivering cheer.
A hedgehog rolls by, quips rolling off fast,
With each playful step, our worries won't last.

The sunlight dapples, flickering bright,
Every turn invites laughter's delight.
A chorus of chuckles rings through the air,
In this joyful place, good vibes we share.

This whimsical journey won't fade away,
As the night falls softly, we continue to play.
Memories woven in this lighthearted maze,
With smiles as our compass, through life we'll blaze.

Swaying with Satire

In the breeze, we sway and jest,
Leaves of laughter, we are blessed.
Tickling trunks with puns so bold,
Whispers of humor, stories told.

Squirrels giggle, acorns chuckle,
Nature's laughter, never a struggle.
Beneath the sun, we frolic and play,
Joyful mischief guides our sway.

Branches dance with playful cheer,
Each rustle brings a grin near.
The sunbeams wink, a witty light,
Tickling minds, a pure delight.

Life's a canopy of witty quips,
Nature's humor in playful scripts.
We laugh with leaves, let worries go,
Swaying with satire, a vibrant show.

The Capering Copse

In the copse where laughter dwells,
Jokes take root like magic spells.
A dance of shadows, witty and bright,
Nature's chuckles echoing with delight.

With each breeze, the branches sway,
Tickling fawns who wish to play.
Mirthful mockery fills the air,
Sudden snorts from creatures rare.

Beneath the canopy, we share our tales,
Of cheeky critters with funny scales.
Foxes grin with playful tease,
Nature's comedy, sure to please.

In this grove of jest and glee,
Spontaneous giggles, wild and free.
A woodland stage where laughs take flight,
The capering copse, a pure delight.

Roots of Raucous Revelry

Down below, the roots entwine,
Hosting humor's grand design.
Beneath the surface, smiles begin,
A raucous revelry from within.

Wiggling worms tell jokes galore,
While mushrooms chuckle, begging for more.
Every root has a story to share,
Of playful pranks and witty flair.

As we dig deep, we find the mirth,
Laughter blooms in earthy birth.
Nature's humor, a timeless sea,
A comedy show under the leafy spree.

From gnarly roots, tales intertwine,
Silly stories that brightly shine.
With raucous revelry, we cheer and grow,
In the rich, dark soil, joy's overflow.

The Comic Canopy

Beneath the leaves, we find our glee,
Laughter dangles from every tree.
With vibrant hues and joyful sounds,
Nature's comedy all around.

Sunlight tickles, shadows play,
A canopy where jesters sway.
Chirping birds, tuning in,
Their cheerful notes on whimsy's din.

The breeze is filled with playful winks,
As leaves rustle in clever links.
Silly squirrels take center stage,
Their acrobatic feats engage.

In this rich expanse of mirth,
Every corner offers fun's rebirth.
Amidst the trees, let laughter reign,
The comic canopy, joy's vibrant vein.

Banter Beneath the Eaves

Under the roof, the jokes fly high,
With every pun, we touch the sky.
Laughter dances like leaves in the breeze,
Tickling noses with whimsical tease.

Whispers of wit, we share a jest,
In the comedy club of our cozy nest.
Chairs creak as we lean and sigh,
Oh, the tales of mischief, oh me, oh my!

Sipping tea, our giggles collide,
Like bees on blooms, we cannot hide.
What's that? A slip, a stumble, a fall?
Just the punchline of a good-natured brawl.

So here we sit, with banter aglow,
The warmth of humor, our hearts all in tow.
Beneath the eaves, we laugh until we bleed,
For joy is the language; all else is just greed.

Sassy Sprouts of Dialogue

In the garden of words, sass takes root,
Sprouting with vigor, oh what a hoot!
A quip from the left, a jab from the right,
We plant our banter, in bloom, what a sight!

Watch the puns twirl like flowers in spring,
Each leaf a laugh, oh the joy it brings.
We chat about life, and all its charms,
With playful nudges and open arms.

From silly slips to playful debates,
Every jest a seed that germinates.
The sun shines brighter, the jokes are lush,
In the rich soil of humor, we laugh and rush.

So let's cultivate this lively exchange,
In the bed of our hearts, nothing feels strange.
With each sassy sprout, our spirits ignite,
In the garden of laughter, everything's right.

Nectar of Nuanced Nonsense

In a world of giggles, we sip the sweet,
Nectar of nonsense, oh what a treat!
With every word, a honeyed drop,
We buzz from glee, we never stop.

Sipping slowly, the laughter flows,
A twist of phrase, oh how it glows!
The jokes are sticky, the puns don't care,
They wrap around us like a warm, soft chair.

Each chuckle's a drip, a teasing taste,
In the jar of joy, there's never waste.
With your wisecrack and my witty refrains,
We brew this pot of playful gains.

So lift your glass, let's toast to the fun,
In this banquet of mirth, the day's just begun.
With nectar so rich, we happily blend,
In this maze of nonsense, the laughter won't end.

The Jestful Roots of Connection

Digging deep, we plant our seeds,
Roots of connection, where laughter leads.
With twists and turns, humor grows,
In this garden of jest, anything goes!

Beneath the surface, giggles entwine,
A network of joy, in the warm sunshine.
The more we share, the deeper we dive,
In the soil of laughter, we come alive!

Quips sprout wildly, like vines they climb,
In the thicket of fun, there's no sense of time.
Every snicker, a petal unfurled,
In the green of good humor, we thrive in our world.

So let's nurture these roots with care and glee,
In this fertile plot, we're wild and free.
Together we grow, the laughter will spread,
For the jestful roots, they never go dead.

www.ingramcontent.com/pod-product-compliance
Lightning Source LLC
Chambersburg PA
CBHW051658160426
43209CB00004B/949